Space E

MW00611821

Contents

Exploring Space

Spacesuits? Check.
Moon boots? Check.
All clear for a moonwalk...

Neil Armstrong was the first astronaut to walk on the moon. He hoped it would help people see that nothing was impossible.

And it did.

Since the first landing on the moon, people have seen spacecraft travel to the outer limits of our solar system. Someday, scientists hope to go far beyond.

A Trip to the Moon

On July 20, 1969, Apollo 11 astronauts Neil Armstrong and Edwin "Buzz" Aldrin were the first to land on the moon. Astronaut Michael Collins orbited the moon in the command module while Armstrong and Aldrin did experiments, collected million-year-old rocks, and raised an American flag.

Astronauts have not been to the moon for over thirty years, but you can still find a lunar rover and footprints on the moon today! Scientists hope to send spacecraft and astronauts to the moon again soon. These missions will help scientists prepare for trips to Mars and beyond.

Planets in Our Solar System

Our solar system has nine planets, which orbit the sun. The outer planets—Jupiter, Saturn, Uranus, Neptune, and Pluto—are hundreds of millions and even billions of miles away from the sun.

Planet	Average distance from the sun	Time to orbit the sun
Mercury	36 million miles	88 days
Venus	67 million miles	7 $\frac{1}{2}$ months
Earth	93 million miles	1 year
Mars	142 million miles	23 months
Jupiter	484 million miles	12 years
Saturn	887 million miles	29 $\frac{1}{2}$ years
Uranus	2 billion miles	84 years
Neptune	3 billion miles	165 years
Pluto	3 $\frac{1}{2}$ billion miles	248 years

Exploring space gives clues to how the universe was formed and how it works. Scientists make discoveries that help people on Earth, too. Exploring space may even show that there is life somewhere else in the universe.

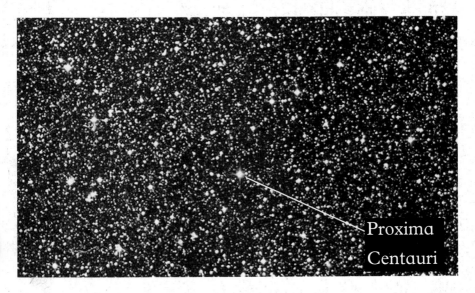

Proxima Centauri

Light travels at 186,000 miles per second. A light-year is the distance light travels in one year. The sun's closest neighbor, Proxima Centauri, is about four and a quarter light-years away.

The easiest way for us to explore space is to just look up! We can peer into a telescope or use a pair of binoculars to get a closer view.

To explore space, scientists use powerful tools such as radio telescopes, satellites, and spacecraft.

Kitt Peak National Observatory in Arizona has a 4-meter telescope in the largest dome.

In the United States, an agency called NASA is in charge of space exploration. NASA's spacecraft have explored every planet except Pluto.

Pluto

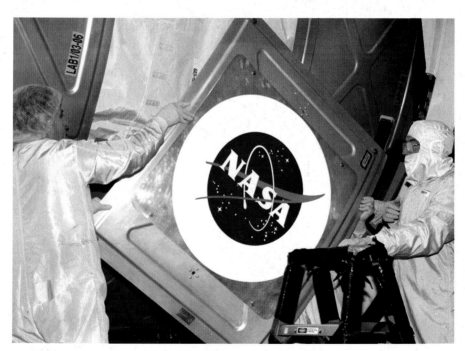

NASA stands for National Aeronautics and Space Administration.

Telescopes

In 1609, Galileo Galilei developed a telescope
and turned it toward the skies. He made
many discoveries with his telescope, including
Jupiter's four largest moons. His observations
confirmed his belief in the theory that the
planets revolve around the sun. Most people
at that time believed the sun revolves around
Earth. Galileo was imprisoned for his beliefs.
It took hundreds of years for people to accept
his ideas.

Galileo

Galileo's telescope

Today, astronomers use large telescopes at observatories to see things that our eyes can't. Scientists also get a view of space from above Earth's atmosphere with the Hubble Space Telescope. This telescope orbits Earth and collects images and other data from far into the universe.

Hubble Space Telescope

Satellites

Artificial satellites are like robots that orbit Earth and do jobs that people can't. Some look into deep space while others look at Earth. They can help find people, warn us about severe storms, and allow us to use cell phones.

A satellite over Earth

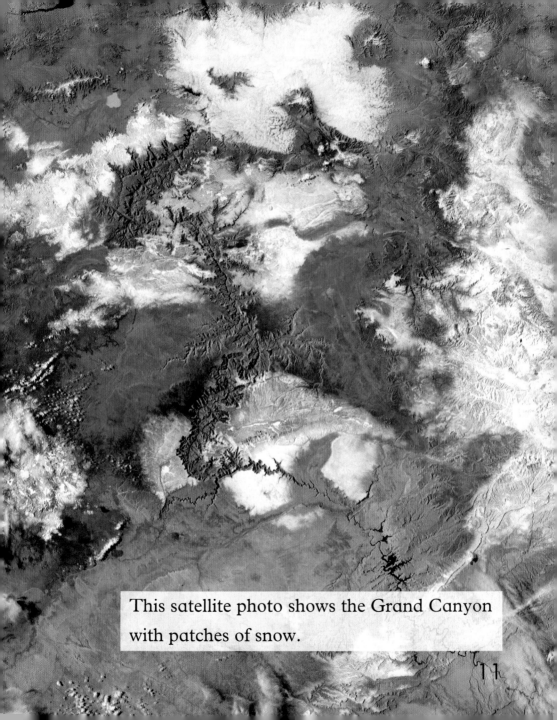

This satellite photo shows the Grand Canyon with patches of snow.

Space Shuttles and Space Stations

Unlike rockets, space shuttles can make many trips into space. Rockets blast shuttles into space, but the shuttles return and land like airplanes. Shuttles have orbited Earth and have allowed astronauts to conduct experiments and repair satellites.

Space shuttles were grounded after the *Columbia* broke apart on its return to Earth in 2003. NASA studied the accident and made plans to send a space shuttle safely back into space.

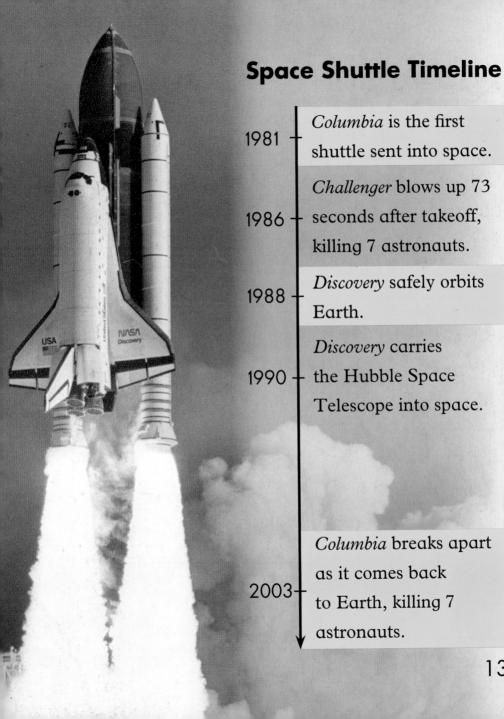

Space Shuttle Timeline

1981 — *Columbia* is the first shuttle sent into space.

1986 — *Challenger* blows up 73 seconds after takeoff, killing 7 astronauts.

1988 — *Discovery* safely orbits Earth.

1990 — *Discovery* carries the Hubble Space Telescope into space.

2003 — *Columbia* breaks apart as it comes back to Earth, killing 7 astronauts.

13

Space stations are places where astronauts can live and work while orbiting Earth. Skylab, launched in 1973, was the United States' first space station. The Soviet space station Mir stayed in space the longest, orbiting Earth for 15 years. The International Space Station is the largest station ever in space. Sixteen countries are working together to build the station. Much of the station has been assembled while it is in orbit.

The International Space Station

Weightless Fun

Astronauts feel weightless in Earth's orbit. They do special things so they don't float all over their spacecraft. They wear a seat belt when they go to the bathroom, and they sleep in sleeping bags that are tied down.

Mission to Mars

NASA sent two rovers, *Spirit* and *Opportunity*, to Mars to search for signs of liquid water in that planet's history. The rovers have studied rocks that appear to have been changed by moving water. Finding signs of water on Mars could mean that Mars once, or still does, support some form of life.

A close-up of the surface of Mars

Mars Exploration Rover

Mars is cold and
rocky and home to
gigantic volcanoes.

Sailing to Saturn

It took the *Cassini-Huygens* spacecraft seven years to travel from Earth to Saturn. It discovered lightning storms and a new ring around the planet. In January 2005, the *Huygens* space probe landed on Titan, one of Saturn's moons. It is the most distant landing of a human-made object in the solar system.

Saturn

Exploring Saturn

The rings that orbit Saturn consist of billions of pieces of rock and ice. They may be the remains of comets, moons, or asteroids that broke up as they neared the planet. *Cassini-Huygens* will fly very close to Saturn and its rings more than 70 times.

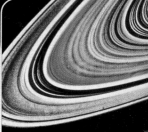

Saturn's rings

Of Saturn's 31 moons, Titan is the largest—bigger than the planet Mercury. It is the only moon known to have an atmosphere, or protective gases, around it.

Titan

Cassini-Huygens is also studying the moon Phoebe. This moon orbits Saturn in the opposite direction of most of its other moons.

Phoebe

Voyaging Beyond Uranus and Neptune

Two *Voyager* spacecraft have been in deep space for 27 years! *Voyager 1* took photos of Jupiter's moons and discovered active volcanoes on the moon Io. *Voyager 2* became the first spacecraft to fly by Uranus and Neptune. The Deep Space Network, which has sets of powerful antennas located in three places around the world, receives information from the *Voyager* spacecrafts.

Uranus   Neptune   *Voyager*

Voyager 1 is now the farthest human-made object in space, and *Voyager 2* is following right behind it. Both *Voyagers* will leave our solar system and continue to send signals from deep space until about 2020.

A Golden Message

Voyager 1 carries a golden record with an audio message to the universe. The recording has sounds of many different things on Earth, including animal sounds, music, and spoken greetings. Scientists hope that someday another life form out in space will listen to the recording.

Space in the Future

Scientists are inventing new ways to travel to space such as solar sails, ion engines, nuclear engines, antimatter spacecraft, and space elevators.

Space exploration answers questions about our universe and helps people on Earth. Do you have what it takes?

Imagination? Check.
Courage? Check.

You are clear for space exploration.

The X Prize

The X Prize was a $10 million contest for a spacecraft built with private funds, instead of government funds. The spacecraft had to carry three people safely to space twice in two weeks to win the prize. SpaceShipOne earned the prize in October 2004 when it traveled $71\frac{1}{2}$ miles into space. Its design may be used to build spacecraft that can take people like you into space.

SpaceShipOne

Index